Pigs

by Peter Brady

FRANKLIN WATTS
NEW YORK • LONDON • SYDNEY

This edition first published in 1998

Franklin Watts
96 Leonard Street
London EC2A 4RH

Franklin Watts Australia
14 Mars Road
Lane Cove
NSW 2066

Original edition published in the United States by Capstone Press
818 North Willow Street, Mankato, Minnesota 56001
Copyright © 1996, 1998 by Capstone Press

ISBN 0 7496 3202 X
Dewey Decimal Classification Number: 636.4

A CIP catalogue record for this book is available from the British Library.

Printed in Belgium

Photographs
The photographs on the cover and pages 4, 8–10 and 18–29 were taken by
William Muñoz, and those on pages 6 and 12–16 were taken by Lynn M. Stone.

Contents

Words in the text in **bold** type are explained in the Useful words section on page 23.

What is a pig?

A pig is a farm animal.
Pigs are reared for food
or to breed more pigs.
A male pig is called a boar.
A female pig is called a sow.

What pigs look like

Pigs have round bodies,
short legs and a curly tail.
They can be black, white,
light brown or spotted.
A full-grown pig usually weighs
about 360 kilos.

Where pigs live

Pigs live on farms.
They are usually kept in special barns.
If they are outside in fields
they have shelters they can go into
if the weather is very hot or very wet.

What pigs eat

Pigs eat their food from **troughs**.
They are usually fed on grain,
but pigs will eat almost anything.
They will eat meat, vegetables, bread
and leftovers from human food.
They can also **digest** grass and roots.

Different kinds of pig

Farmers have kept pigs
for hundreds of years.
Now there are more than
300 different **breeds**.
The names of some of them are
Large White, Gloucester Old Spot,
Landrace and Tamworth.
Farmers mix breeds
to get better tasting meat.

Clever animals

Farmers say pigs are
the cleverest of all farm animals.
If there is a hole in the fence
around their field
they will quickly find it and escape.
They have a good sense of smell
and can root out things underground
with their **snout**.

Mud

Pigs lie in mud in order to keep cool.
Because they cannot sweat as we do,
they get hot very quickly.
Pigs can also get sunburnt
because they do not have much hair
to protect their skin.

Piglets

Sows are usually pregnant for
three months, three weeks and three days.
They give birth to between
eight and twelve piglets.
When it is born a piglet
weighs about 1.35 kilos.
Six months later
it will weigh 99 kilos.

What pigs give us

Pigs give us meat which is
treated in many different ways.
Bacon, ham, sausages and pork
all come from pigs.
Their skins are used to make leather
for gloves, shoes, bags and coats.
Surgeons use **valves** from pigs' hearts
to replace diseased ones in human hearts.

How to make a piggy bank

What you need
    1 litre plastic jug or similar container with a lid
    four small paper cups   pink felt
    one pink pipe cleaner   glue
    marker pen

What you do
1 Turn the jug or container on its side. The lid will be the pig's snout. Have the handle on top if you are using a jug.
2 Glue the cups to the bottom of the jug to make the pig's legs.
3 Cut the felt into triangles. Glue them to the top of the jug to make the pig's ears.
4 Ask an adult to make a small hole in the end of the jug. Push the pipe cleaner into the hole and twist it to make the pig's curly tail.
5 Draw the eyes above the snout with a marker pen. Now the bank is ready.

To put money in the piggy bank just take off the lid.

Useful words

breed   group of animals with the same ancestors

digest   to change food into something the body can use

snout   another word for a pig's nose

trough   long narrow container used to hold food or water

valve   small flap in blood vessels that makes blood move round the body in one direction only

Books to read

First Discovery: Farm Animals, Moonlight Publishing, 1996

Food from Dairy and Farmyard, Young Library, 1985

King Smith, Dick, *All Pigs are Beautiful*, Walker Books, 1993

See How They Grow: Pig, Dorling Kindersley, 1992

Index

PRINTED IN BELGIUM BY
proost
INTERNATIONAL BOOK PRODUCTION